Gut

Gut

Amanda Larson

OMNIDAWN PUBLISHING

OAKLAND, CALIFORNIA

2021

Cover photo by Hannah Thornhill
Taken on September 14, 2018 in Uluwatu, Bali

Text set in Baskerville MT Pro

Cover design by Amanda Larson
Interior design by adam b. bohannon

Library of Congress Cataloging-in-Publication Data

Names: Larson, Amanda, 1997- author.
Title: Gut : poems / Amanda Larson.
Description: Oakland, California : Omnidawn, 2021. | Summary: "Amanda
Larson's Gut interrogates the agency of a young, female speaker in the
wake of trauma and desire. Larson places feminist theory in conversation
with personal experience in order to examine the impact of such forces
on traditional ideas of logical agency. The book moves through Larson's
recovery while questioning the limits of the very term, and of language
as a whole. She employs a variety of different forms, including prose,
Q&A poems, and a timeline, to do so, that reflect both the speaker's
obsession with control, and her growing willingness to let it go. In
this way, Larson's measured voice paves a way for how we can continue to
live despite what happens to us in the process"-- Provided by publisher.

Identifiers: LCCN 2021032384 | ISBN 9781632430977 (paperback)
Subjects: LCGFT: Poetry.
Classification: LCC PS3612.A77344 G88 2021 | DDC 811/.6--dc23
LC record available at https://lccn.loc.gov/2021032384

Published by Omnidawn Publishing, Oakland, California
www.omnidawn.com   (510) 237-5472
10 9 8 7 6 5 4 3 2 1
ISBN: 978-1-63243-097-7

To my friends at Scripps College,
who taught me how to be beautiful, and what it meant

CONTENTS

II: SPRING

Pain always produces logic, which is very bad for you.

—FRANK O'HARA

When I return, the sun hooks my flesh and raises it, exposes me like a cowhide rug; the oaks of campus engulf me in their strong, hairless arms. I do not know what could be called *joy*, if it is this movement, or anything else. Signing a book I bought, a poet asks *where are we?* and I say *I have no idea, we are in California, somewhere*, the shadow of the palms blanketing our bloated flesh.

●

There is no word in English for the sensation of water covering your being, of the loss of gravity experienced when immersed, a nerve-ending reversal.

●

I've discovered this sensation could occur just by covering one's mouth with another. I've discovered that this could happen for years. Men would lift me by the chest as a child, and the vertebrae would crack into place upon the removal of my own weight. We did this together for years.

●

If there is a condition of being used, it is in the muteness that follows the crack, in the humming that remains.

●

A piece called "The Angel of Progress" warns of calling this spring a moment of ending, of calling it anything other than what it is. *I wish to question...a singular, monolithic term, organized around a binary axis of time rather than power.* There's a danger here of premature celebration, that the language I use is empty appearance.

●

You could say that about the terms: *recovered, recovery.* You could say that about a lot of things. Like when I say *my body,* as if it is not work to believe the use of the possessive.

●

It itches, *recovery*, the implication that something was lost. I maintain no desire to be the person I was before abroad, the person who allowed those things to happen to me.

●

The only poems I wrote in the fall, when those things happened to me:

One of wanting to be murdered, one of the desire to deny pleasure, given that I was so starved for it and took what I could get.

Q: If you are alone, at what point is this an advantage?
At what point are you measuring threat?

A:

A way to begin is with the Men of E. One cannot speak of these things without mentioning them. The Men obtain their name through a dream in spring, method by which they would not approve. In it, I am in a grocery store of E's. I find my father, and the Wound-Watcher, and a boy I will call only E., because that is his name. *Are you the Man of E I am in love with?* I ask all three, waltzing from aisle to aisle, the fluorescent lights pouring off eggs.

No, each Man of E says, and I wake up despondent, in grey light.

As a child I could always be found in a serious relationship, a translucent girl on a red cloud, not knowing how I got there or why I was even there in the first place.

•

Moments I was jerked into consciousness by fear. At seventeen in the cloth passenger seat of a car, with the prickly faux-velvet material sticking to the underside of my thigh: a man is taking me into the woods; he wants to go for a walk. A pack of cigarettes stares at me from the plaqued cup holder. He is twenty-three years old, my manager at work, and irritatingly hungover. *What am I doing?*

•

At twenty I see an author speak; see a girl ask her about the processes of unlearning. *How can one unlearn?* The author is swift. She castigates the past as if it were a hangnail to be ripped from the thumb. *No point in unlearning!* she jaws. *The only way to bring justice to the past is for the past to never have happened.*

•

When she said this, and again when I am told that this author is known to be a cruel person, I am reminded of one man's ability to cut people out of his life, brutally and immediately, for the sake of preserving his own autonomy. I am reminded that this ability is why I return to him, the Man who Watches the Wound.

•

Stalking home from E.'s room one early night a year ago, the moon the white of an eye, my mind is fighting the thought that I don't like this person at all, E., whose room it was, E. who I have declared I am with.

But I would not bend over for him, and that is what I do like, the movement of his body through the line of control. Never again to mutter: *It's whatever, it's whatever's fine with you!* I cannot remember a word he said; it's a new sensation, a relief I will misinterpret as freedom.

•

I could shackle myself to another to rid myself of temptation. I could do, really, whatever I wanted.

•

I think about those things that happened and how they changed that girl on that walk, who was so deliberate and paced in her being. I think about the function of shock. Cathy Caruth explains it another way: how to return unwillingly to a traumatic event is not an attempt to re-witness or understand it, but rather an attempt to reinstate proof that you can survive timelessness, what trauma effectively creates.

●

I like this timelessness because it throws away logic, which stung. Logic cannot render the vulnerabilities of my body impervious—they glared in the context of what others saw after, underneath the polyester of a useless pantsuit.

●

Eve Sedgwick states that paranoia moves similarly, *backwards and forwards in time.* For *there must be no bad surprises, and because learning of the possibility of a bad surprise would, in itself, constitutes a bad surprise.*

●

What distinguishes an explanation and a warning?

●

At times E. is still there when I close my eyes; I speak to him. This is the only time I articulate the reality of my pain, where the act of arguing produces a reality I can stand being in. I picture E. laying down next to me, a bulk of gallant mass, who can not only protect me, but wants to.

●

The argument was so clear. Silent, it lasts for hours. *I am sorry*, I start, imagining my face wet and panting, as if exposed to steam; *I am so sorry*. In real life I say it to him only once; it does not work.

●

My father spoke to me during abroad but I don't recall how. At one point I messaged the Wound-Watcher asking how he had motorcycled around Tanzania the year before, and ended up in a town consisting entirely of coffin makers.

●

The timelessness is the result of a puncturing fright. Cathy contends that bodily wounds were, on occasion, a sure sign one's psyche would come clean from the war, forcing the afflicted into a concrete reality.

●

I lost ten pounds and I cannot gain it back. There were no full-sized mirrors when I was there, only a six-inch one in which I could track the status of individual parts. A pointed hip here, breast there, the white stomach diminishing into a long, abandoned road.

●

You can't compartmentalize the past so long as you survive, author. *If the dreams and the flashbacks of the traumatized thus*

engage Freud's interest, it is because they bear witness to survival
that exceeds the very claims and consciousness of the one who
endures it.

•

But I understand the appeal. If I could, I would take my
survival conscious.

•

That is to say: I would function under certain deliberateness,
a type that I could remember and understand. I would not
have called E. at 5:30 in the morning after another man
had tried to rape me. I would not have done it regardless
of the sky, how it was then, the color of a bloodied gum.

Q: Did you know it was your body before you touched it?

A:

I remember my palm smothering my brother's abhorrent mouth.
Younger, he was too much, oblivious to the faces of others,

and there was never a time where I was. His body was seamless,
running feral with the pack of boys who coveted our grass,

and my envy articulate, acute. Early, I understood
how women were kept in rooms; worse,

how frequently it was the result of their own volition. Early,
I sharpened spears in my backyard,

the sticks thinning under the rush of the sharp rocks,
the trees puckered from the amputation of limbs.

I could press them to my brother's neck if I wanted;
I could kill an animal if I wanted. But I never did,

or I don't remember. What I remember is knowing pleasure
at the sight of my shirt hiked up to my breasts,

the smoothness of the stomach that revealed itself at seven.
I don't remember a time where I wasn't doing that; lifting my shirt

and checking my width, my hands cleaving the fat. Even then, I knew
I could have a particular type of power; that soon,

I would let anyone touch me
in the same way I did myself.

Last summer I taught children how to read. I taught them the difference between a long and a short vowel. *Cap, cape, slat, slate. The difference, boys and girls, is E.*

●

If I could, I would hold my mind with the discipline of these Men. Sometimes I imagine it: being totally consumed by a work, and it is a joy to do so, to occasionally dip my head below the water. I imagine how they do not consider me at all, existing outside the realm of my own self-consciousness.

●

Patricia Hill Collins understands the standard of such dichotomy: *Research methods generally require a distancing of the researcher from his or her "object" of study by defining the research as a "subject" with full human subjectivity.* But there was no one moment I can remember where I, or she, was not being looked at.

●

I imagine how I would occur to a man in this state. *You know I approach intimacy differently,* the Wound-Watcher once chastised me, and I found it riveting, the idea that even this, he could control.

●

A second requirement is the absence of emotions from the research process. In vinyl photographs, a hand is dripping down my back, growing lower until it reaches a tipping point; in the grocery store, a man pushes his cart from aisle to aisle, follows me until he stops, and greets me with distinct breath.

●

That was how E.'s mind was then, and remains today. I held onto his goodness for so long. It blew up in the presence of the man who did those things to me, magnified as a microscopic image, a cell giving way to a deranged shield of white on the pupil, and with my hands erratic around the zooming knob: I looked, and drowned.

●

His silence was cyclical in nature, drew me towards him. It served as evidence of a complete devotion to his work, one that I could never fully achieve, despite my effort, sweat. I was a scarecrow, watched and mangled by black beaks: he was the farmer, standing whole in the endless field.

●

And I remember: translucent girl, red cloud, she whose desire reached until it snapped.

Q: But you must have known the shape of a night?

A:

Usually there's a pack of glossed co-eds,
their smiling jowls bared, cackling as if hyenas
who have gained a whiff of prey;

but tonight, they're gone. Rather,
two of us speak as we shuffle our feet across the blades
of black grass, the night pregnant,

and circling. Ahead, a blonde squares her steps.
Light funnels out from a room on the corner of a dorm,
out of a building I call motel-style, coated with unhinged

orange doors. Inside, we see Maya's body,
buoyant on a rancid couch, her body enveloped in sweatpants,
and a young man standing in front of her, laughing

as she jumps, circus-like. The blonde
notices, turns towards the light, like a mosquito,
deluded. She croons; *You guys just look like you are having so*

much fun. Like, so much fun. Have
a good night. She leaves. Maya laughs. Her boyfriend nods.
I spent all of last year trying to get other people

to like them. My friend purses her lips,
our arms knit as we walk farther. We are going to a party, curious
if we can make the most of it. Then, she asks, *do you think our darkness*

is fundamentally different from Maya's darkness?
The question isn't of presence. We know, logically,
Maya's experienced something, life, has fallen or failed, tasted loss;

know that the silent poses she holds in the photographs online do
not represent who she can be. Still, my voice is anxious, my friend's
a tone I rarely encounter. It is not the acknowledgement of the act

by that impetuous blonde, either. We agree on this—
how many times each of us could recount
our stomach stretched out in the backseat of a car,

or a forced unconscious laugh, erupting
from the feeling of a thumb pressed to the throat.
Once we reveled in it. Now,

we have questions of fundamentals,
of the use of our bodies in the creation of guilt.
There's a stinging desire in the drugged air,

and we both feel it, then: the hauling eyes of the moon.

On the last trip we took together, E. and I had sex no fewer than two times a day, once up to five, no longer capable of speaking to each other. But it felt good to do that, to be beautiful for a time and nothing else, to capitulate. *The weapon and the tool may seem, at moments, indistinguishable,* Elaine Scarry writes in *The Body in Pain.*

●

To be treated as an entirely physical form—as that man did, the night when those things happened to me—by which I mean treated me as something non-living—made me feel as if I must have eliminated something that, though I had repressed before, I had never mutilated, or destroyed.

●

Having grown older, and experienced that splitting desire—I had been trying to separate the body and mind, then, wanting to be more-than-woman, a creature of pure will, proving I could have some utility.

I realize, now, he wanted to do the same thing.

●

I had to ask who it was that was missing, there, who it was that I was, to demand that he see something human, my

arms flailing, borderline comedic. I wanted to know what
it was, in me, that allowed for that to happen.

•

Gillian Flynn, on the continued presence of sexual assault
allegations: *They hate us. That's my immediate thought, with
each new revelation: They hate us. And then, a more sick-making
suspicion: They don't care about us enough to hate us. We are
simply a form of livestock.*

•

Did I not deserve that?

I invited him back. I intended something animalistic. And
the line is very, very thin.

Q: Did you love him (E.), or were you given?

A:

E. was like the men of the looming houses I grew up in, the men whose teeth were sharpened bone. I remember the clink of those teeth against crystal, how they spoke of the scandal of lawn, its determined verdant.

●

There is a way about how the word love echoes when it is said back, like a molar of doubt, demonstrating the debt incurred.

I used to not speak of desire; I spoke of myself as changed and independent, though I did not change, or could not. Susan Bordo can speak of anything, too. When writing her dissertation, she critiqued the idea of duality in a male mind and female body. She relied only on male sources, a mistake she recognizes twelve years later, in 1992. *I still expected "theory" only from men. Moreover—and here my inability to "transcend" these dualisms reveals itself more subtly—I was unable to recognize embodied theory when it was staring me in the face.* There are some things, in doing, we cannot be expected to say.

●

The Wound-Watcher is the first person I sleep with in spring, after those things happen to me—knowing that if I collapse, he would never tell anyone.

●

I like sleeping with him, like sleeping with his friends, the way I can trust and endure them. They draw out a kiss like a cloth from my mouth and then bleed into the background of my life.

●

What type of recovery is this?

●

I need them to prove that those things would not happen to me each time I let a man touch me. It is still a function of need.

●

Works that perform such abstraction and elaboration get taken much more seriously than works which do not. Susan sees things for what they are, though I am in no place to make an argument for what, exactly, that is.

●

Patricia advocates in *Black Feminist Thought* for similar forms of embodied theory, that which she reclaims in order to pursue a community-oriented mode of justice. But I never asked if these men were in on it.

●

In the wake of after I tell one to do mushrooms, not with me, but alone, stating plainly that it will give anyone the feeling of being in love. *But I don't want that feeling,* he replies. The yellow walls of my room linger as sweat on a pale cheek. And it was so strange to me, for he treated me with such care.

●

Anne Carson contests: *Written texts make available the notion that one knows what one has merely* read. Plato was particularly concerned about the advent of the text for this reason, believing that knowledge was something to be necessarily obtained through living *in space and time.*

●

In space and time, there is a way I can present myself that mimics knowledge, or maybe even is it, as in, I know how to act to get a good man to sleep with me, I know how to present my interests, to laugh, the angle at which I can cock my head to the side. On campus I know where they linger, who I can contact. It's comforting, the idea that I know anything at all.

●

But there were always objects outside of my grasp: my eyeliner smudged, the pat of blush too heavy, the discursive glance of another who is equally deserving. I admit that I'm writing what happened now to impose control. Hélène Cixous still believed it to be impossible: that writing is a free-for-all form of erotic exercise, no control guaranteed.

●

One girl in my class could not write an E. She mangled it constantly, rendering a distorted "3." She is old enough to know better, and yet I don't know what that means; I corrected her, furiously.

●

Hélène believed every word she wrote to be ample examination of what it is she was writing. As in before, I had regarded the body as the only thing that was honest in its wanting.

●

Walking back from the Wound-Watcher's room after sex, earlier than daybreak: I pass swimmers going to practice, their male bodies enveloped in hooded garments, each the color of blood. The fabric stalks about their protruding knees. My shirt is mesh under my crossed arms, and the night limits what I can see to only what is in front of me, proves it suffocates all else.

Q: What type of recovery is this?

A:

It was these men who rendered you expert:
Your diverting eyes, thrash of hip, chin raised

in mechanical indifference. At one point, even,
another man, his hand down your pants

in public. You win. What else are you supposed to say,
with a lack of bodily injury. What are you supposed to say, at all.

There is nothing worth doing if you do not feel cute,
a woman, a feminist, tells you.

Half of the recognition you got at all was physical.
Look at you there, twirling your beautiful hair—

a man, a Professor, says of you in class.
Granted, you were doing that,

looking so slack-jawed and indolent.
If things are as they appear, you capitulate,

you self-sustain like any live thing:
in the movement of your body appearing across the floor.

In the gradual reveal of her navel,
the newfound shock of your tongue.

When Anne writes of desire, she does not write in gender, but rather the lover and the non-lover, the desirer and the desired. For her, fear of possession is legitimate; desire splits and splits, gives ways to deluge. *Is melting a good thing?*

●

In which case, the flood is something that happens to you, upon you. I don't recall that sensation when I when I was younger: I remember capitalizing on absence, speaking of those other than myself, lowering a risk. It was good, there, to be defined by a man, to be wavering at a grey-lit bar at sixteen, my being confirmed by the sheathe of his palm stitched to the small of my back. That was what my love looked like, Anne. It was not the same for him.

●

For there to be a flood, there must be a landscape that is flooded, fields to be clogged and relics to be ruined, but I did not have a house, or a landscape. I feared another so wholly that I would become whatever it was they wanted.

●

Whenever I see the Wound-Watcher, it is always for the first time in several months. One time I see him and tell him how dormant my summer has been—every day the children, my family, the uses of E. He replies, *Oh. You want to talk to me to focus on a life other than your own.*

I am so drawn to men who speak to me like this, men who take a concealed desire, and lay it out clean.

•

Concealed implies that I knew of this and took steps to hide it, but really I cannot say if I knew it or not. What matters the most is the movement, the sleight of hand that creates the revelation. I remember everything he said; the Men of E remind me there are things I do not know within me, however cruel they may be.

•

Writing her dissertation *eros the bittersweet*, Anne maintained the potential of an indulgence. The Other, according to her, creates a heightened sense of self that is equivalent to a feeling of godliness, fueled by the eyes of the beloved. It is all dependent on the space between us. *Union would be annihilating*, Anne warns.

•

Can you only be annihilated once?

•

Or can it happen multiple times, a continual process? I would have done anything to keep those men around. And I did do anything, with no convincing; I simply wanted to.

Q: The night of, the televisions broadcasted a story of the fires in California. The leaves and the branches appeared on fire, culminating in the trunk, the forest, and then an entire town.
Can you only be annihilated once?

A:

A burn is a singular event, manifested on the flesh; its change is linear and permanent. The image of the fire recurs, a constant.

I am reading *The Newly Born Woman* by Hélène when I see the author speak. At twenty, I'm engrossed by her, Cixous, her scintillating utterances of the cosmic libido. She writes of the fear of possession as a masculine fear; declares positively, *She is not able to return to herself…she is not the being-of-the-end (the goal), but she is how-far-being-reaches!*

●

But what do you do if it is terrifying to move?

●

A night out in a crowded bar in Edinburgh, the men breathing on my collarbone in rotation. One, older, comes too close, paws his hand into my hip. I shoot my thin elbow into his gut, but the impact of the tired bone is minimal; his drunk body lurches on to another, dumb. My friend sees me, narrows her brow, goes *Jesus.*

●

The only way to bring justice to the past is for the past to never have happened. As if it's easy, to heal in the mode of forward thrust. To not speak to your family for thirty years, as the author I saw did. It's tempting, the clean break into your own autonomy.

●

That's just how men are, my mother would say. I want to believe otherwise, but there are rooms I want to know where silence settles upon the arrival of my body, as frost does glass.

●

As if, in not speaking to them, she could erase them from her consciousness entirely. If I am not-speaking to someone, I am certainly speaking of them; the fact of our not-speaking creating a new morsel of thought in and of itself, melting away a sickly pink on my drenched, rabid tongue.

●

Did you ever consider, a friend asks, that you may not have actually been doing anything that crazy? That you never stalked him, berated him, never called him more than twice in a night?

No, I respond.

●

Meeting after he has been backpacking in foreign lands, I see the Wound-Watcher's teeth shear meat off a rib, as if the death of the animal were dependent on his mouth. Better, in his eyes, for both.

Q: But what do you do if it is terrifying to move?

A:

Imagine in your past you had written words on the page, words like *desire,* or *Other,* or *E,* you had written these words and done so like a fact, with the clean nose of grammar and a derivable meaning. Such indications are used to demonstrate proof. Yet when you read the words now, the marks are there but they do not mean the same thing. They do not mean the same thing, at all. But you wrote them down, they are there. They even won an award.

Language is like the balancing act of my body on the rim of an in-ground swimming pool, with the concrete on one side and water on the other. I can see the liquid rendered by compulsive waves, and the concrete oblique, controlled—sometimes my mind gives way to vertigo. Sometimes I fall, and drown, or break open my temple on the stark ground, watch scarlet blood heave onto the earth.

●

At times I don't want to put words to what happened. I begin running, spinning, in erotic, long stretches, holding my mind in a corporeal state, the sun aching over my glistening body through the metallic shrapnel of the gym.

●

My mother howls through the phone: *You can never get over anything!*

And I am falling, falling, knowing that I have lost all markers of such, and may not have had them in the first place.

●

The markers being what's said: articulated proof of my well-being or progress. What resulted from my pain was not a loss of language, a cone of silence punctuated only by moans, as described by Elaine in *The Body in Pain*— but a loss of meaning, the knowledge that whatever

I said could never truly communicate; a fear of mine
from the beginning, and the reason I write at all. *Drown.*

●

Is this pain the only thing I have to myself?

●

On one hand, the language boiled: you saw a madwoman
with a frenzied tongue, horrified of what her silence might
reveal. On the other hand: I could say, really, whatever I
wanted.

●

Occasionally what happened appears in my mind like a
flat, startling image—but mostly it is these words, rushing
from some unholy source. *Perhaps trauma victims are more
concerned with not thinking of it.*

●

Example: on the phone with my mother, who is telling
me that she does not want me to get a job I applied to
on Cape Cod because I cannot handle it, being up there
all alone, the salt air mutilating my lungs and my body
untouched. *Just like Scotland,* she says. Furious, I hang up,
and go to get coffee: in the shop, E. and his new girlfriend,
sitting together, looking at me with their small eyes.

●

The words arrive, all the comments about her appearance, her literacy level, the complacent way she is always adorned (this is true) in his sweats for his chosen contact sport. As if he has to dress her in the morning! I have written letters to her under the guise of warning, mouthed to my friends about her, thought of her with potent urgency.

And when I know what I cannot speak; my mind twists to the bodily, struck by desire to pour my iced latte on her, to do it slowly, with precision and control, to see the liquid infiltrate her nostrils, to witness her wither under the soak of milk. I am shaking, shaking, the latte dribbling.

Part of me wants her to be touched as I was.

But I would never do that. So I walk out of the coffee shop, and into the open air.

•

For consciousness, survival does not seem to be a matter of known experience at all. I have never handled it well, this unable-to-speak into being.

•

When I see her when I'm drunk, I'm known to whisper frantically to my friends: *Can she read? Can she read?*

•

What do I do, Hélène, if the rage takes over my language, too? How do I write the body if what is written is a horrified thing?

●

These moments of rage characterize spring. They are useful because they are moments, and not the general state of being I was in months before: shocked each night by the perpetual, wasp-like return of the emotion, my palm grasping for the knob of the lamp, searching, again, for the smother of light.

●

I know the things that I said to E. and his new girlfriend because I know their angle, the hot point of the blade in which the words took their etch, and yet a year later I cannot remember them, at all.

Q: What is the body writing?

A:

All your poems mention men or sex, the Wound-Watcher critiqued. Like all of his didn't, as well.

●

I tell him it's a privilege to articulate the need in terms of a want. The last night I slept with him, Sam warned me of what I said, protests of the act, giving way.

I have a strange feeling about tonight, she went. *I have a feeling there will be a lot of moving parts.*

●

I knew I was going to do it before I did it.

How badly I wanted some part of me to be understood as decadent, or unforgivable.

When I was reading, it was so easy for me to be happy, Roxane Gay writes in her memoir *Hunger,* on her immersion into literature after her rape. But this is a notion I have strived against all my life—the idea that in books or in writing I could impose some type of control; that I would have to turn to them for that type of control. I did not want that. I wanted a world in which I could argue my way out; though I always felt what she said to be true.

•

Before those things happened to me, I had been trying to argue my way out.

•

As a lover you want ice to be ice and yet not melt in your hands. As a reader you want knowledge to be knowledge and yet lie fixed on a written page. Anne constructs the paradox, that for one to know something is only worth it or proven through living it, and exposing its lack as a result. I have learned that there was no reality in which I could argue my way out.

•

E. had straight white teeth and a credible résumé, a way of speaking about things in a calm, low tone. I do not remember a word he said, but I remember his voice, how it sunk and caught as we approached sleep.

•

I wanted to be like him—adhering to a standard that he'd never questioned, pliantly following desire at it appeared. The last trip we took together was the only time I felt it: we climbed a cape that loomed over the Pacific, positioned our bodies on the precipice. I hung to his arm through layers of pilled fabric and watched as the velvet waves coerced the rock, as the salt air mottled our cheeks— after those things happened, I remembered the walk with meticulous detail. It became a constant, the only thing I wanted to return to.

But he did not love me anymore, and so I did not think I could go back.

●

I take much comfort in agoraphobia, that there are those to whom their fears align with their actions. I take much comfort in the reversal.

Q: What are your choices?

A:

Barbara Johnson writes that *Female logic, as she defines it, is a way of rethinking the logic of choice in a situation in which none of the choices are good.*

You are, you were, sanction
from the suffocating lights of the bars,
and the grimace of clubs, each deaf-dumb beat

shuddering through my walls,
a room where my limbs are kept
wool-coated and splayed. My phone's glow

runs empty and dull, your mouth absent teeth—
Your silence that of a sickening drum.
My jaw is clenched. It has stuck right through

since the day where I had done things;
and had to do them for you:
I spread his tobacco on the table,

to rid the evidence of him from my room.
I remember the look as I did it,
in morning, my body strange and bruised.

I told on him, then, to you. I said: *these things never
go away.* And I remember with every thud of smoke
that comes through my window, rising

from Cowgate below, locked in the bedroom
where he split my body, two hands, crisp fruit.
I do not sleep, his flesh wrung free,

your silence that of a sickening drum.
You do not like your women used.
But he is outside; he knows where I *live*—

There are things you know
that you cannot know.
The sun sinks at three. I do not see blue.

I've always found humor in pain. Like sitting around my kitchen table as a teenager, my parents either stoic or seething, my mother holding some impenetrable knowledge. At seventeen, I would embark on these long, irritating monologues, just to break the silence, to see what comes out of it. *I have taken many lovers—*

●

I begin to covet. One: a podcast of two women, speaking of the murders of primarily women. I listen to them when I travel alone, my sweating flesh exposed within the fluorescent, plastic cartridges of public transport. Their words render me conscious of my full display to illegible men. But it's their voices that I find soothing; a clear expression that the anxiety I experience about my body, or what could be taken from me, is not mine alone.

●

If I like nothing else, I like this podcast, and a pair of black leather boots I bought in the wake of everything— studded with silver, a flare on the heel: if I can do nothing else, I can wear them. I want to determine what would define me if I went missing; rather than suspects, I want a place I would be seen last, some object preoccupying my hands.

●

Not the same as it was before, concerned with if my wants were the right wants, the right way to make this body turn out. I've learned there is no right way: no one way that will render it safe.

●

I don't know if I would have listened to the podcast years ago. I speak of and read everything I found repulsive before: these female writers, made sick from desire, hoarding their skirts and walking into the ocean. *Discrimination between the imaginary and the real can only be made through behavior,* Simone de Beauvoir writes. I now know they are no longer pretending. Rather, they simply feel.

●

Reading the poems of Anne Sexton, he approaches me with his own book, asking to join. When I tell him *I'm just hanging out with Anne,* he goes *That's funny; she can't enjoy hanging out with you,* and sits.

●

I attempted, before, to achieve recognition for lack-of recognition, for a lack-of care, a heightened sense of intellectual purity. I am no longer interested. It was not what kept me alive.

●

Like you could build a will from a set of ribs. Or a woman from one.

●

I'm tired of pretending I'm anything besides a haphazard being that validates the concern about the weaknesses of her sex. Like looking gawk-eyed and useless in the Madrid airport, my tank-top strap broken, sprinting to a flight. The man working in customs stalls me by singing *Sevillaaaaa, Sevilllaaaaas so beautifullll, you're so beautifulllll,* and I don't scream, I let him, knowing what he would have believed if I had opened my mouth, anyway.

●

Before, I would have screamed. But I know, now, there's no use in pretending that I don't need him to let me through.

●

I don't mean this in terms of capital; in terms of saying that you should be complacent in order to get ahead, to obtain his validity. I'm simply trying to understand picking one's battles as a legitimate and necessary part of a lived female experience, one that before, I had fought against vehemently.

●

Like the way that men will buy you drinks. Nights I don't want them to at all; but I don't view their presence, anymore, as hindrance to buying your own, or to the silk of the night, the way the painted faces of your friends shine adoringly in the thick of a wooden bar. The men will always be there, watching, their eyes rendering you all a presentation, or, for some, prey.

●

Still, I remember how the bills shriveled in his greased palm.

●

I remember the eyes of his friend more, though, the night those things happened to me. They were adorned with a bright, flickering orange. She grabbed my face between her palms, and, with the smell of cider wavering, went: *you're absolutely lovely, aren't you?*

III: SUMMER

Each to his grief, each to
his loneliness and fidgety revenge.
Nobody knew where I was and now I am no longer there.

—GWENDOLYN BROOKS

I begin to write. When Mary Ruefle is asked about how her gender impacts her writing, she replies, *the simplest I can put it is to say this: my life is the struggle between bodies (minds with minds) while my writing is the struggle between mind and what is without mind.* In the latter, she is referencing death, that which she refers to as *the highest end of the wiring.*

•

Mary suggests a level playing field, brought on by mortality; a gesture I can appreciate. But it bears too much correlation to the politics that denies how certain bodies are not brought closer to death simply by the fact of existing, living, in those bodies. Death can be a matter of proximity: just ask Cathy and her description of timelessness, that death-like state.

•

The pieces I write result in a deluge of messages along the lines of *Jesus Christ, are you okay?* sent to me on Facebook at two in the morning, from individuals I hardly know.

•

You won't like his work, someone says to me at a reading. *It's very abstract, there's no structure, you won't like it.*

I'm okay with no-structure! I protest. He looks at me again, eyes of tepid blues. *You fucking hate no-structure.*

•

The poet reading is a man, old and white, and one of his poems is just him saying the word "Bird" forty times.

●

How I have always feared the white underside of my father's iris, the space below his pupil as his eyes drift up into his head.

Q: Were you alone?

A:

The woman's breath crowded her tongue. This I know.
How I have lived in the muteness of the home,

how I came to language slowly, learning injury
in my mother's mouth flicking

and giving way to more, the words fixing argument,
then carving out my bones.

I spoke when I was spoken to, countered,
moved from the state of being watched

to watching. It's futile, then: the memory of a man
teaching me to punch in the corner of a bar, *as if you are spilling*

a cup of coffee, or shutting myself in a basement,
splitting my muscles under the strain of black machines.

But Virginia, these conditions are far from perfect—
the distinction between hostility and indifference

is that indifference never had a mouth.
I whet mine in hostility's wake: spent summers reading

while the hot blank metal of a chair imprinted into my skin.
I would peel an orange back to membrane,

enmesh its pulp in my teeth.
Watch as the juice went running, then was left

on my wrist, on my mutilated thumb;
left anxious, there, for the tongue of the dogs.

There is something passive in the mind that cannot be willed simply by speaking. I know this from experience, and from Maggie Nelson's book *Bluets*, which examines the gap between *knowing* and *believing*.

●

That's just how men are, my mother would say. When those things happened I was wearing a shirt exposing the entirety of my ribs, I did not know him; *knowledge,* that I did not wield tactfully.

●

But to *wield* that knowledge feels like allowing my hand to grasp the wrong end of the knife. I will not deny myself certain joy, that which Frank O'Hara knows, of showing *a rib-cage to the rib-watchers.*

●

There are different things I know and believe. One does not necessarily correlate with another. At times I believe that men are good, or bad; I know that men are good, or bad. Nights I set up narratives, and let the narrative play out.

●

Any movement resists the stability of categorization. I like the feeling of his knuckle underneath my chin as he raises it and asks, *do you want to leave?* All I can feel is my body distending over its wants.

Q: What do you want?

A:

There are three dogs. Three dogs breathing their excess against the door, each one a different color and each one exhaling the same milky fog. It is June, bad night, and my skin is mosaicked with flecks of brown, my temple pressed to the other side of the glass. The dogs aren't hungry tonight, that's what I think, and that if they are, you can't tell. You can't tell until the moment they eat, the moment when it happens. Outside light streams in through the door, hitting the corner of my eye; it's always been filtered, filtered through the glass, and, more importantly, through what comes from their jaws.

●

Mostly, I want this fear to dissipate.

In Paris, I am mute as we walk around the water lilies, all those blue flowers Claude painted in the wake of the war. I picture him sitting, for four years, silently moving his brush, as my grandmother had once circled her palm on my child back, drifting into sleep beneath the hum of the fan, coated in artificial dusk-light.

And I think: if there is not an ending to this state, there could be, at least, something to be gained in the attempt of one.

●

That afternoon, I purchase a notebook with the water lilies on it. Lauren goes: *I love that—we just saw all these beautiful flowers, and now you're going to put all your beautiful thoughts in that notebook.* And I love that she said that, though what happened had just happened two weeks ago, and I was speaking, then, in tongues.

●

It was a moment of something else breaking through.

A moment, knowing: if there is a part of me that has been untouched by others, I haven't met it.

●

It has always been desire outpaced by other desire. How it looked that July: spent beneath a man with indigo eyes, our lungs swollen with heat, bodies sheathed only by the beige, sweating walls. To ask what I wanted more than him was like asking what you could want more than to eat. What, starving, could you want more than the food placed, in moments, on your very tongue. I wrote physical lists, heaved my body into books: I shackled myself in solitude to blank plains of grass, read about desire, how it could look outside of him—

I knew what I told myself, and when he did not want me, it proved to be true.

●

There's still terror, though, of what could have happened if he had. What I could have given.

I still find pleasure in the story, and so when I am asked of that summer, it is what I say. No word of what I wrote or read—though those too, were movements—but rather the feeling of my body in smoldering heat. An image of the field on fire, that which I could not distinguish from the field, or the fire.

Q: What can you endure?

A:

Later, my mother will say, *it is not the pain,*
but the anticipation of it—

Now, it is not my duty to help.
My cousin's screams reverberate

as the sun does through the leaves,
shifting over my collapsed body, limp

on a plastic raft. I cannot see her skin, bloodied,
or the gnarled earring that punctures it,

the heavy green gut of the buddleia obstructing.
From behind it, my aunt waltzes:

her slim body appearing,
disappearing, the screams quivering

then plunging. She will not be able to touch.
Like my cousin, I kept a defensive throat.

I was told this as she will be,
and she will swallow it just the same—

with the memory becoming the throat,
and then her body, limp on a plastic raft,

drifting across this pool.
In one week, I will be twenty-one years old;

I must have become something other
than what I was told I was.

The evaporating brick makes contact
with the skin of my foot, and I begin to drift,

again, the pattern made dull.
For years I convulsed at the others I did not want—

When I was younger I was desperate to be hurt
in any way that would be believed.

We take a trip to a beach in Mexico, a fifteen-hour bus ride to a stone town on the coast. Kaila and Sam, two of my close friends, are there. Their irises are porous, and brown as silt.

•

We spend long nights speaking of love, with questions of want: how it exists in the presence of rage, consolidated. And I no longer care if what's real is what is projected onto us—these depressed women from a liberal arts college, meant to be "empowered," caught up, again, in speaking about men, their parents, the look of their fathers. I feel close to them beneath the flickering lamps of that filthy room on the beach, our words as constant as the croon of the ceiling fan.

•

Sam says, *No, no, she was manic.* Says, *I saw the rage rush over her, her eyes filled black.*

She's talking about me.

•

Without judgment, the speaking is as satisfying, as compulsive, as a tongue running over a gum where wisdom teeth bloom. The words begin to snag, again, begin to hold their meaning.

•

What is the use of a tool when, in using, it changes its form?

•

But there's just no way for things to be left clean, my body slowly beginning to accumulate weight. What Anne Sexton said functions almost as compulsion: *I am queen of all my sins / forgotten.*

•

Rather than a self, the movement forward what is kept constant—and what is forgotten, moving it along. *You just don't know what motivates people,* I say. *You just don't know.*

But of course, I do know, I knew it all along. I had hands and I wanted to do something with them. But who was I to think I could will grace, that which Eve states it is necessary to leave room for: *because there can be terrible surprises, she writes, there can also be good ones.*

●

That summer I felt my skin as sheathed by the tight expanse of a bathing suit, how the sand stuck to my skin and rolled off it, I couldn't seem to lose the small grains of stone, finding bits of them everywhere, digging through my hair with the hook of a fingernail, and coming up with the small, glistening parts.

●

I lose track of the Men of E. They occur to me fleetingly, as I do to them.

●

I swim with Susan through clear, sharp waves to a black rock off the coast, where a tide pool of water is nestled, ivory films of salt floating on its surface. Occasionally we drag our fingers through the delicate, filthy crystal, watch as it drifts apart. Our thighs meld to the rock; I tell her how, before, I could not shake the memory of him, how my mind revolved around that thought, and, sitting with her, my friend for years—I told her I wanted this one to replace it. I cannot say if it did or did not.

Forgetting is, indeed, a necessary part of understanding, Cathy writes. Eventually I stop speaking of what happened; I reintroduce silence. I don't know where the words went. At some point, I must have put them down.

Q: What is the use of a tool when, in using, it changes its form?

A:

There was a woman once with whom I spoke about my production value. I spoke to her every Thursday, walking my body over to her office and settling it down on her plush couch. *Perhaps,* she would say, stirring her tea and putting it to the side, *you deserve [x] because you are a human being, and because you are alive.* My timelessness did not seem to occur to her. Rather, she had decided, that regardless of what one experienced, they could, at the least, believe in a linear pattern, believe in a cause and effect, a bell and a reward. I had once believed this too, except I had worked for it, worked to be the bell, but when I could no longer do so, what mattered was that there was an award anyway, which was, I was alive.

In movies the moments of joy are condensed to montage, success is played out over the course of three minutes. To spend any longer on it is to endure risk: that of stagnancy, or boredom. But I feel now the privilege of no longer enduring such immediacy of experience, to forget the palm that rested on the back of my neck.

In moments I can even lose the memory of its feeling. When explaining his poem, "You Are Jeff," Richard Siken states, *everyone in the world—including the speaker and the reader—is named Jeff. With only one identity, each part of the world must now define itself in relation to its other parts, rather than as a stand-alone thing, independent of context.*

After those things happened to me, this became abundantly clear—that even with the blind light of the sun piercing through my eyelids, I would consider him.

●

Take, for example, three dogs at home and I am with my mother, in a sterile house by the beach. My father's family has taken its shift for the week, and its windows are wide, a view of the steel ocean constantly pouring in. My relatives circle as my mother rouges the raw meat with breadcrumbs, immerses the cuts in a bubbling, crimson sauce. I know they want; but she has always taught me how to work when watched, and, in doing so, to create a mode of joy.

In August, I move into a house. It is filled with light. Of course, at times the house was very dark. At times it was no color at all. But it has been a year since those things happened, and I want to allow myself this: the sun illuminating dust, its heat independent, and palpable. I want to allow myself to name it, while admitting that to name it is, at times, to lie.

•

In the house I live with a friend, but in living with her, I do not live with her—I live alone. Not to say she is never present; she is, frequently, and we will speak for hours, our words punctured by strange, cyclical laughter. But I have known her for so long: I effectively live alone. She is so close to me that she is a part of it. If someone were to ask me about her, I wouldn't know what to say.

Q: Do you want to forget?

A:

I am breaking from old patterns and moving on with my life, bell hooks writes in her book *all about love,* and I repeat this to myself to the extent that it becomes a new pattern, and though it may reference the old—it is a different movement. I do not want to go there, again, and yet I know I may—this knowing will not prevent me from doing so. *I am breaking from old patterns and moving on with my life.*

Before, I made certain choices in certain environments so I felt better in those environments, around those people. When those things happened to me, those people were gone, and all I could see was the stout red curtains of my bedroom, embossed by a nauseating print, one from the decade before I was born.

●

I know what I said: *I maintain no desire to be the person I was before, the person who allowed these things to happen to me.*

●

But I try to follow Joan Didion's advice. What she says: *I think we are well-advised to keep on nodding terms with the people we used to be, whether we find them attractive company or not. Otherwise they turn up unannounced and surprise us, come hammering on the mind's door at 4 a.m. of a bad night and demand to know who deserted them, who betrayed them, who is going to make amends.*

●

Who is going to make amends?

●

I thought in the past that when women spoke of those things, they were, in fact, *seeking attention.* I never admitted it, thought it only to myself, but remember the prevalence of doubt in my tone as I spoke. It lingered in me then, as smoke darkens the sinus.

●

It is present in the first words of the book: *the person who I was before, the person who allowed those things to happen to me.*

Part of me must have figured that was what you wanted to hear, what you would find pleasure and security in: that such a person could exist.

●

I maintain no desire to be the person who I was before.

But, like language, it is hard to establish difference from the past without spite, to say *There are no definitive statements about who I am now,* without rendering a definitive statement that overturns everything else that came out of my mouth. I don't know if there is such a thing as letting go; I know what can be said of me, what can be resurrected. But I no longer let such fear eclipse my future—and I am not the same person I was before, who allowed it to do so.

When I drank on that trip I woke up in a fervor, early, in a manic state. I went to a hammock and laid in it as the sun shed its palms over the horizon, dying the water pink, and rendering myself a nude, tropical bird, lying in the midst of a pile of plucked, effervescent feathers.

●

It could be her that does it, that makes things right: with the beauty of life blanketed plain across her view.

●

But I worked once at a photography agency, convinced I would be content with assisting in the creation of beautiful things. The workload was high, and the moments were short, with thousands of images to be sifted through each day. I wanted more time.

That was the summer I went mute: working in silence
with all those images plastered around me, and dating E.,
his furrowed brow. I thought it could make me happy, to
be detached from language, that which forced me to be in
places other than where I was.

●

It was before those things happened to me. One poem I
wrote that June: on my house, burning.

●

You can dress your mouth however you want, smear it
with an intoxicating gloss—but what comes out reveals its
undercurrent.

Q: Who is going to make amends?

A:

It hit me as I was driving home at night from New York,
a strange longing for California, its egregious sky

rendered by smog, bright pink like a mouth
speaking something it wants. I wanted

to fear a person the way I did there; for that was, there,
the smallness of my life: I feared one person, a man;

I was horrified of what he thought of me, watching
as I turned my small leased car into my apartment,

how he could see that nothing was my own.
E. had loved me so much that he hated me;

he hated that he could not tell the story apart from the way it was told,
and I told too many stories, I could sense myself like that, infringing.

He was a child of film. He spoke of it like an infection,
and I remember agreeing, in a way I do not acknowledge.

Before I met him, I was planning to move to Los Angeles,
telling everyone who asked, *it is so fake there, it's real.*

But I met him and pictured a child staring
at the great white plastic of the Hollywood sign,

amongst the houses that were the color of eyes,
how everything there was always at risk of burning—

I could not. There were ways that I could categorize myself,
language that collapsed my life into a film reel, entire swaths of it

denigrated to *justs*. Just college, just the years I was West,
just one night under his palm, in the lamp-lit room.

I was thinking of California, and how I was running out of justs,
that soon the sun there would settle into a mocked, electrical night,

and that this would be my life.

The way I act is different from the way I acted a year ago. I cannot demarcate when or how that happened, or if the previous words and actions dribbled off, like drool from the mouth of a drunk.

●

I still drink and go out. I like to see the things that escape my mouth when I am not thinking about the things that escape my mouth, how I grow inclined to press my bare shoulder against the animal tongue of a brick. Months go by where I leave with no one, walking home alone in the night, my path lit by the orange glow from the fragrant, occupied rooms.

Desire has always been this convoluted. Even, years ago, with his body standing Christ-like in the perforated water, the herons surrounding like ordained guests, even with his finger tracing the scarred inside of my thigh—there was still what it was the coursed through his veins, the drugs, and the potential for cruelty. Part of me knew, and part of me ignored it, because I wanted something to be consumed by, and I was, I felt like I was, consumed.

●

But what I remember changes depending on the present. Like my teenage years—I used to believe it was only the men I could recall, but now I know there was a general state of being young and alone, in bed with my body illuminated, hums of music keeping me awake.

Because the reader has room to realize that the future may be different from the present, it is also possible for her to entertain such profoundly painful, profoundly relieving, ethically crucial possibilities that the past, in turn, could have happened differently from the way it actually did, Eve writes. When I was there I spoke frequently with my mother about whether or not I could go home, an idea I never pursued before or one that had ever brought me much comfort. *But what are you going to do at home?* she would ask.

I had no idea, no notion of what it was my life could resemble—I responded that I wanted to read books in my room.

●

At times the past appeared a physical thing, as in Carrie Fountain's poem *yes,* where the past is a person, *coming, catching up, hands caked with dried mud, head shaved clean.*

●

But he cannot not touch me anymore. That summer I immersed myself in the thick, navy waves of the Atlantic, and allowed my body to be carried to shore.

Siken goes: *Let's say the Devil is played by two men.* I used to have dreams of men with black curly hair on the side of a road, the back of their heads facing towards a verdant field. I wrote poems about them years ago, ones that repeated the phrase *we're done for, we're done for.*

●

But who could define that? I was never actually done for; I could never actually become them. Each attempt left residue, a scrap of paper, which I picked up and plastered together to make something resembling the silhouette of a self, a body in low light.

In the middle of my hometown there's a road that cuts through several acres of tall, warm grass, disrupted by a single house. It has remained that way for years, the acres untarnished and wavering in a sinking sun. I wanted to run through them as a child and I could never, horrified that the property was not my own.

●

Regardless, I am no longer there.

●

Regardless—before the train from New Jersey dips into the tunnel of New York, there's a marsh of navy blue pools, haloed by cord grass. From the car, the train appears to be drifting on water. And it is a miracle that someone could do that: could meld the tracks by shoveling dirt and sand in a line through the vista, the tunnel by bombing underneath a city—and, in doing so, create a mode of tangible progress.

●

I have looked out onto it my whole life, and knew what it meant to be moving.

●

Knew what it meant to throw my body against another, whole or in parts, to feel what's inside rushing to the skin, the membrane diminishing. Brought on by a glance.

●

I can only know my eyes as they are when looking; my brow as fixed, and wanting.

●

I: FALL (TIMELINE)

June 5, 2017: Accepted to a political internship in Edinburgh, Scotland.

August 28, 2017: Flight from EWR to EDI

October 2017: Event

November 2017: Meeting with program coordinators

November 2017: Title IX report filed by coordinators

November 2017: *ultimately it is the man you mentioned who would have to approve your early departure from the program...you can ask for flexibility but can't dictate they provide it.*

November 2017: Appointment scheduled with therapist, in Edinburgh.

November 2017: *he will be in a position to confirm whether or not your early departure will impact upon him and the team.*

November 16, 2017: Thanks for checking in. I did have a conversation with Prof. _____ about leaving early but I found therapy to be helpful and have decided to not further pursue it. I think to do so would be to allow what happened to define my abroad experience. I am now leaving three days earlier, December 13 instead of December 16,

December 2017: 2,500 word report completed on Broadband Provision in rural Scotland.

December 13, 2017: Flight from EDI to EWR

I had such bad jetlag. The vomit pooled in small paper bags, and remained for two weeks, my head lingering, then stuck, inside the toilets' white rims.

January 2018: Flight from EWR to LAX

NOTES

On page 12, *"I wish to question…a singular, monolithic term, organized around a binary axis of time rather than power"* is a quote from "The Angel of Progress: Pitfalls of the Term Post-Colonialism" by Anne McClintock, published in the journal *Social Text,* by Duke University Press in 1992.

On page 15 and 17, The sections on Cathy Caruth are paraphrased from her book *Unclaimed Experience: Trauma, Narrative, and History,* as published by Johns Hopkins University Press in 1996.

On page 16, "paranoia moves similarly, *backwards and forwards in time. For there must be no bad surprises, and because learning of the possibility of a bad surprise would, in itself, constitutes a bad surprise."* is a paraphrased quote from Eve Kosofsky Sedgwick's essay "Paranoid Reading and Reparative Reading, or, You're so Paranoid, You Probably Think this Essay is About You," as it appears in her book *Touching, Feeling: Affect, Pedagogy, Performativity,* published by Duke University Press in 2002.

On page 17 and 18, *"If the dreams and the flashbacks of the traumatized thus engage Freud's interest, it is because they bear witness to survival that exceeds the very claims and consciousness of the one who endures it."* is a quote from Cathy Caruth's *Unclaimed Experience.*

On page 21, *"Research methods generally require a distancing of the researcher from his or her "object" of study by defining the research as a "subject" with full human subjectivity."* and *"A second requirement is the absence of emotions from the research process."* are quotes from *Black Feminist Thought* by Patricia Hill Collins, published by Routledge Publishing in 2000.

On page 25, *"The weapon and the tool may seem, at moments, indistinguishable."* is a quote from *The Body in Pain: The Making and Unmaking of the World* by Elaine Scarry, published by Oxford University Press in 1986.

On page 26, the Gillian Flynn quote is from an article published on December 6, 2017 in Time Magazine, titled "Gillian Flynn: A Howl." Accessible at: http://time.com/5050757/gillian-flynn-on-women-speaking-out-sexual-harassment/

On page 28 and 29, *"I still expected "theory" only from men. Moreover—and here my inability to "transcend" these dualisms reveals itself more subtly—I was unable to recognize embodied theory when it was staring me in the face"* and *"Works that perform such abstraction and elaboration get taken much more seriously than works which do not."* are quotes from "Feminism, Foucault, and the Politics of the Body" by Susan Bordo, as it appears in *Feminist Theory and the Body, A Reader*, edited by Janet Price and Margaret Shrildick, and published by Routledge Publishing in 1999.

On page 29 and 30, *"Written texts make available the notion that one knows what one has merely read."* is a quote from quotes from *eros* by Anne Carson, published by Princeton University Press in 1992.

On page 33 and 34, *"Union would be annihilating"* and *"Is melting a good thing?"* are quotes from *eros* by Anne Carson.

On page 36, *"She is not able to return to herself...she is not the being-of-the-end (the goal), but she is how-far-being-reaches!"* is a quote from *The Newly Born Woman* by Hélène Cixous, as published originally in France as *La Jeune Née* by Union Géneral d'Editions, Paris, in 1975, and translated and published in English by the University of Minnesota Press in 1986.

On page 40: *"Perhaps trauma victims are more concerned with not thinking of it."* is a quote from Cathy Caruth's *Unclaimed Experience*.

On page 41, *"For consciousness, survival does not seem to be a matter of known experience at all."* is a quote from Cathy Caruth's *Unclaimed Experience*.

On page 44, *"When I was reading, it was so easy for me to be happy"* is a quote from Roxane Gay's memoir *Hunger*, published by Harper Collins in 2017.

On page 44, *"As a lover you want ice to be ice and yet not melt in your hands. As a reader you want knowledge to be knowledge and yet lie fixed on a written page."* is a quote from *eros* by Anne Carson.

On page 46, *"Female logic, as she defines it, is a way of rethinking the logic of choice in a situation in which none of the choices are good"* is a quote from Barbara Johnson's article "Apostrophe, Animation, and Abortion," as published in *The Barbara Johnson Reader* by Duke University Press in 2014.

On page 49, *"Discrimination between the imaginary and the real can only be made through behavior"* is a quote from *The Second Sex* by Simone de Beauvoir, originally published as *le deuxième sexe* by Éditions Gallimard, Paris in 1949, and later translated and published by Vintage Books in 2011.

On page 55, *"the simplest I can put it is to say this: my life is the struggle between bodies (minds with minds) while my writing is the struggle between mind and what is without mind."* is from Mary Ruefle's essay "Lectures I Will Never Give," as published in her book *Madness, Rack, and Honey* by Wave Books in 2012.

On page 67, *"I am queen of all my sins / forgotten."* is a quote from Anne Sexton's "You, Doctor Martin," as appears in *Selected Poems of Anne Sexton*, published by First Mariner Books edition 2000.

On page 68, *"because there can be terrible surprises, she writes, there can also be good ones."* is a quote from Eve Kosofsky Sedgwick's essay "Paranoid Reading and Reparative Reading, or, You're so Paranoid, You Probably Think this Essay is About You."

On page 69, *"Forgetting is, indeed, a necessary part of understanding."* is a quote from Cathy Caruth's *Unclaimed Experience*.

On page 72, The Richard Siken quote is from Legacy Russel's interview with Richard Siken, as published on October 11, 2011 in Bomb Magazine. Accessible: https://bombmagazine.org/articles/fight-club-richard-siken/

On page 75, the Joan Didion quote is from her essay "On Keeping a Notebook," as published in *Slouching Towards Bethlehem*, as originally published by Farrar, Straus, and Giroux in 1968.

On page 84, *"Because the reader has room to realize that the future may be different from the present, it is also possible for her to entertain such profoundly painful, profoundly relieving, ethically crucial possibilities that the past, in turn, could have happened differently from the way it actually did"* is a quote from Eve Kosofsky Sedgwick's essay "Paranoid Reading and Reparative Reading, or, You're so Paranoid, You Probably Think this Essay is About You."

On page 84, *"coming, catching up, hands caked with dried mud, head shaved clean"* is a quote from Carrie Fountain's poem "yes," as it appears in her volume *Instant Winner*, published by Penguin Publishing in 2014.

On page 85, *"Let's say the Devil is played by two men."* is quote from Richard Siken's poem "You are Jeff," as appears in his volume *Crush*, published by Yale University Press in 2005.

ACKNOWLEDGMENTS

I'm grateful to *The Adirondack Review,* who published the contents of "Q: Did you know it was your body before you touched it?" and "Q: Were you alone?" in their Summer 2019 issue, and to the Mellon Foundation and the New York State Summer Writer's Institute, whose grants and scholarships allowed me to begin writing this project in the summer of 2018.

Thank you to my parents and my grandparents, for your support and incessant belief.

•

Thank you to all the children I have watched, taught, and nannied during the process of writing this book. I hope your lives are everything I promised they would be.

•

Thank you to all the Professors of the Scripps College English department (the Miller Wing). Special thanks to Professors Michelle Decker and Warren Liu, whose classes, at a time of intense uncertainty, made it abundantly clear what I could do with my life. This book would not exist without your careful reading and guidance.

•

Thank you to my teachers in writing, and in this project: Henri Cole, Warren Liu, Sarah Manguso, Adam Novy, Matthew Dickman, Sharon Olds, Anne Carson, Major Jackson, and Ed Hirsch.

•

Thank you to my peers in the NYU MFA program, who read my poems and challenged them.

•

Thank you to everyone at Omnidawn, and to Jericho Brown, for reading this and understanding.

•

Thank you to those who I have lived with in the past three years: Nora Dell in Scotland; Sam Martin, Meghan Grewal, Callie Walsh, Lauren Shoemaker, Bella Ratner, and Sofia Padilla in California, and Becky Novik and Nell Bailey in New York. I write with you around me always. Also, thank you for the parties.

•

Thank you to Sam Martin and Sandro Ortega for being some of the first readers of this book, and for your friendship.

•

Thank you to Sena Cebeci for the conversations that helped shaped this book and my life.

•

Thank you to Emily Meltzer, Susan Chen, and Becky Novik, for being with me in New Jersey and ever since.

•

And thank you to Rob, for all of it.

ABOUT THE AUTHOR

Amanda Larson is a writer from New Jersey, and a graduate of Scripps College in Claremont, California. Her writing has appeared in the *Michigan Quarterly Review, Washington Square Review,* and other publications. She is currently an MFA Candidate in Poetry at New York University.

Gut
Amanda Larson

Cover photo by Hannah Thornhill
Taken on September 14, 2018 in Uluwatu, Bali

Cover and interior typeface: Baskerville MT Pro

Cover design by Amanda Larson
Interior design by adam b. bohannon

Printed in the United States
by Books International, Dulles, Virginia
On Glatfelter 50# Cream Natures Book 440 ppi
Acid Free Archival Quality Recycled Paper

Publication of this book was made possible in part by gifts from
Katherine & John Gravendyk in honor of Hillary Gravendyk,
Francesca Bell, Mary Mackey, and The New Place Fund

Omnidawn Publishing
Oakland, California
Staff and Volunteers, Fall 2021

Rusty Morrison & Ken Keegan, senior editors & co-publishers
Kayla Ellenbecker, production editor & poetry editor
Rob Hendricks, editor for *Omniverse*, marketing, fiction & post-pub publicity
Sharon Zetter, poetry editor & book designer
Liza Flum, poetry editor
Matthew Bowie, poetry editor
Anthony Cody, poetry editor
Jason Bayani, poetry editor
Gail Aronson, fiction editor
Laura Joakimson, marketing assistant for Instagram & Facebook, fiction editor
Ariana Nevarez, marketing assistant & *Omniveres* writer, fiction editor
Jennifer Metsker, marketing assistant